MznLnx

Missing Links Exam Preps

Exam Prep for

Intermediate Algebra

Sullivan, Struve, 1st Edition

The MznLnx Exam Prep is your link from the texbook and lecture to your exams.
The MznLnx Exam Preps are unauthorized and comprehensive reviews of your textbooks.

All material provided by MznLnx and Rico Publications (c) 2010
Textbook publishers and textbook authors do not particpate in or contribute to these reviews.

MznLnx

Rico
Publications

Exam Prep for Intermediate Algebra
1st Edition
Sullivan, Struve

Publisher: Raymond Houge
Assistant Editor: Michael Rouger
Text and Cover Designer: Lisa Buckner
Marketing Manager: Sara Swagger
Project Manager, Editorial Production: Jerry Emerson
Art Director: Vernon Lowerui

Product Manager: Dave Mason
Editorial Assitant: Rachel Guzmanji
Pedagogy: Debra Long
Cover Image: Jim Reed/Getty Images
Text and Cover Printer: City Printing, Inc.
Compositor: Media Mix, Inc.

(c) 2010 Rico Publications

ALL RIGHTS RESERVED. No part of this work covered by the copyright may be reproduced or used in any form or by an means--graphic, electronic, or mechanical, including photocopying, recording, taping, Web distribution, information storage, and retrieval systems, or in any other manner--without the written permission of the publisher.

Printed in the United States
ISBN:

For more information about our products, contact us at:
Dave.Mason@RicoPublications.com

For permission to use material from this text or product, submit a request online to:
Dave.Mason@RicoPublications.com

Contents

CHAPTER 1
Real and Algebraic Expressions — 1

CHAPTER 2
Linear Equations and Inequalities — 5

CHAPTER 3
Graphs, Relations, and Functions — 11

CHAPTER 4
Linear Functions and Their Graphs — 14

CHAPTER 5
Systems of Linear Equations and Inequalities — 17

CHAPTER 6
Polynomials and Polynomial Functions — 20

CHAPTER 7
Rational Expressions and Rational Functions — 25

CHAPTER 8
Radicals and Rational Exponents — 29

CHAPTER 9
Quadratic Equations and Functions — 33

CHAPTER 10
Exponential and Logarithmic Functions — 36

CHAPTER 11
Conics — 39

CHAPTER 12
Sequences, Series, and the Binomial Theorem — 42

ANSWER KEY — 44

TO THE STUDENT

COMPREHENSIVE

The *MznLnx* Exam Prep series is designed to help you pass your exams. Editors at MznLnx review your textbooks and then prepare these practice exams to help you master the textbook material. Unlike study guides, workbooks, and practice tests provided by the texbook publisher and textbook authors, *MznLnx* gives you **all** of the material in each chapter in exam form, not just samples, so you can be sure to nail your exam.

MECHANICAL

The MznLnx Exam Prep series creates exams that will help you learn the subject matter as well as test you on your understanding. Each question is designed to help you master the concept. Just working through the exams, you gain an understanding of the subject--its a simple mechanical process that produces success.

INTEGRATED STUDY GUIDE AND REVIEW

MznLnx is not just a set of exams designed to test you, its also a comprehensive review of the subject content. Each exam question is also a review of the concept, making sure that you will get the answer correct without having to go to other sources of material. You learn as you go! Its the easiest way to pass an exam.

HUMOR

Studying can be tedious and dry. MznLnx's instructional design includes moderate humor within the exam questions on occassion, to break the tedium and revitalize the brain

Chapter 1. Real and Algebraic Expressions

1. In plane geometry, a _____ is a polygon with four equal sides, four right angles, and parallel opposite sides. In algebra, the _____ of a number is that number multiplied by itself.
    a. Thing
    b. Square1
    c. Undefined
    d. Undefined

2. _____ is a document with an outline and summary of topics to be covered in a course.
    a. Syllabus2
    b. Thing
    c. Undefined
    d. Undefined

3. _____ are strategies and methods of purposeful learning, usually centered around reading and writing.
    a. Thing
    b. Study skills3
    c. Undefined
    d. Undefined

4. _____ refers to tasks assigned to students by their teachers to be completed mostly outside of class, and derives its name from the fact that most students do the majority of such work at home.
    a. Homework4
    b. Thing
    c. Undefined
    d. Undefined

5. Mathematical _____ is used in mathematics, and throughout the physical sciences, engineering, and economics. The complexity of such _____ ranges from relatively simple symbolic representations, such as numbers 1 and 2; function symbols sin and +, to conceptual symbols, such as lim and dy/dx; to equations and variables.
    a. Notation5
    b. Thing
    c. Undefined
    d. Undefined

6. A _____ is a symbolic representation denoting a quantity or expression. It often represents an "unknown" quantity that has the potential to change.

Chapter 1. Real and Algebraic Expressions

a. Variable6
b. Thing
c. Undefined
d. Undefined

7. In mathematics, a _____ may be described informally as a number that can be given by an infinite decimal representation.
   a. Real number7
   b. Thing
   c. Undefined
   d. Undefined

8. _____ is an inexact representation of something that is still close enough to be useful. Although approximation is most often applied to numbers, it is also frequently applied to such things as mathematical functions, shapes, and physical laws.
   a. Approximating8
   b. Thing
   c. Undefined
   d. Undefined

9. _____ is the mathematical operation of combining or adding two numbers to obtain an equal simple amount or total.
   a. Thing
   b. Addition9
   c. Undefined
   d. Undefined

10. The _____ is a mathematical symbol used to indicate equality.
    a. Equal sign10
    b. Thing
    c. Undefined
    d. Undefined

11. An _____ is an equality that remains true regardless of the values of any variables that appear within it, to distinguish it from an equality which is true under more particular conditions.

Chapter 1. Real and Algebraic Expressions

  a. Identity11
  b. Thing
  c. Undefined
  d. Undefined

12. In philosophy, mathematics, and logic, a _____ is an attribute of an object; thus a red object is said to have the _____ of redness.
  a. Thing
  b. Property12
  c. Undefined
  d. Undefined

13. In mathematics, a _____ is the end result of a division problem. It can also be expressed as the number of times the divisor divides into the dividend.
  a. Thing
  b. Quotient13
  c. Undefined
  d. Undefined

14. In mathematics, the _____ is the least common multiple of the denominators of a set of vulgar fractions.
  a. Lowest common denominator14
  b. Thing
  c. Undefined
  d. Undefined

15. In mathematics, _____ is a property that a binary operation can have. Within an expression containing two or more of the same associative operators in a row, the order of operations does not matter as long as the sequence of the operands is not changed.
  a. Thing
  b. Associativity15
  c. Undefined
  d. Undefined

16. An _____ is a function that does not have any effect: it always returns the same value that was used as its argument.

a. Thing
b. Identity function16
c. Undefined
d. Undefined

17. The mathematical concept of a _____ expresses the intuitive idea of deterministic dependence between two quantities, one of which is viewed as primary and the other as secondary. A _____ then is a way to associate a unique output for each input of a specified type, for example, a real number or an element of a given set.
   a. Thing
   b. Function17
   c. Undefined
   d. Undefined

18. _____ is a mathematical operation, written a^n, involving two numbers, the base a and the exponent n.
   a. Exponentiating18
   b. Thing
   c. Undefined
   d. Undefined

19. In mathematics, a _____ of a k-place relation $L \subseteq X_1 \times \ldots \times X_k$ is one of the sets X_j, $1 \leq j \leq k$. In the special case where k = 2 and $L \subseteq X_1 \times X_2$ is a function $L : X_1 \to X_2$, it is conventional to refer to X_1 as the _____ of the function and to refer to X_2 as the codomain of the function.
   a. Domain19
   b. Thing
   c. Undefined
   d. Undefined

Chapter 2. Linear Equations and Inequalities

1. The word _____ comes from the Latin word linearis, which means created by lines.
   a. Linear1
   b. Thing
   c. Undefined
   d. Undefined

2. An _____ is a mathematical statement, in symbols, that two things are the same or equivalent. Equations are written with an equal sign, as in 2 + 3 = 5.
   a. Thing
   b. Equation2
   c. Undefined
   d. Undefined

3. A _____ is a symbolic representation denoting a quantity or expression. It often represents an "unknown" quantity that has the potential to change.
   a. Variable3
   b. Thing
   c. Undefined
   d. Undefined

4. _____ is the mathematical operation of combining or adding two numbers to obtain an equal simple amount or total.
   a. Thing
   b. Addition4
   c. Undefined
   d. Undefined

5. The _____ states that if the same number is added to each side of an equation, the results are equal. That is, if x = y, then x + z = y + z.
   a. Addition Property of Equality5
   b. Thing
   c. Undefined
   d. Undefined

6. In philosophy, mathematics, and logic, a _____ is an attribute of an object; thus a red object is said to have the _____ of redness.

a. Thing
b. Property6
c. Undefined
d. Undefined

7. In mathematics, the _____ is the least common multiple of the denominators of a set of vulgar fractions.
a. Thing
b. Lowest common denominator7
c. Undefined
d. Undefined

8. An _____ is an equality that remains true regardless of the values of any variables that appear within it, to distinguish it from an equality which is true under more particular conditions.
a. Identity8
b. Thing
c. Undefined
d. Undefined

9. A _____ is an abstract model that uses mathematical language to describe the behavior of a system. Eykhoff defined a _____ as 'a representation of the essential aspects of an existing system which presents knowledge of that system in usable form'.
a. Mathematical model9
b. Thing
c. Undefined
d. Undefined

10. A _____ is a special kind of ratio, indicating a relationship between two measurements with different units, such as miles to gallons or cents to pounds.
a. Thing
b. Rate10
c. Undefined
d. Undefined

11. _____ is a physical quantity expressing the size of a part of a surface. The term can also be used in a non-mathematical context to be mean "vicinity".

a. Thing
b. Area11
c. Undefined
d. Undefined

12. _____ is the distance around a given two-dimensional object. As a general rule, the _____ of a polygon can always be calculated by adding all the length of the sides together. So, the formula for triangles is P = a + b + c, where a, b and c stand for each side of it. For quadrilaterals the equation is P = a + b + c + d. For equilateral polygons, P = na, where n is the number of sides and a is the side length.
   a. Perimeter12
   b. Thing
   c. Undefined
   d. Undefined

13. In geometry, a _____ is defined as a quadrilateral where all four of its angles are right angles.
   a. Rectangle13
   b. Thing
   c. Undefined
   d. Undefined

14. In plane geometry, a _____ is a polygon with four equal sides, four right angles, and parallel opposite sides. In algebra, the _____ of a number is that number multiplied by itself.
   a. Thing
   b. Square14
   c. Undefined
   d. Undefined

15. In mathematics, a _____ is a quadric surface, with the following equation in Cartesian coordinates: $(x/_a)^2 + (y/_b)^2 = 1$.
   a. Thing
   b. Cylinder15
   c. Undefined
   d. Undefined

16. In mathematics, a _____ is the set of all points in three-dimensional space (R^3) which are at distance r from a fixed point of that space, where r is a positive real number called the radius of the _____. The fixed point is called the center or centre, and is not part of the _____ itself.
   a. Thing
   b. Sphere16
   c. Undefined
   d. Undefined

17. The _____ of a solid object is the three-dimensional concept of how much space it occupies, often quantified numerically.
   a. Thing
   b. Volume17
   c. Undefined
   d. Undefined

18. In geometry, an _____ is a point at which a line segment or ray terminates.
   a. Thing
   b. Endpoint18
   c. Undefined
   d. Undefined

19. _____ is the state of being greater than any finite number, however large.
   a. Thing
   b. Infinity19
   c. Undefined
   d. Undefined

20. In elementary algebra, an _____ is a set that contains every real number between two indicated numbers and may contain the two numbers themselves.
   a. Interval20
   b. Thing
   c. Undefined
   d. Undefined

21. _____ is the notation in which permitted values for a variable are expressed as ranging over a certain interval; "5 < x < 9" is an example of the application of _____.

Chapter 2. Linear Equations and Inequalities

a. Interval notation21
b. Thing
c. Undefined
d. Undefined

22. Mathematical _____ is used in mathematics, and throughout the physical sciences, engineering, and economics. The complexity of such _____ ranges from relatively simple symbolic representations, such as numbers 1 and 2; function symbols sin and +, to conceptual symbols, such as lim and dy/dx; to equations and variables.
   a. Thing
   b. Notation22
   c. Undefined
   d. Undefined

23. In mathematics, a _____ may be described informally as a number that can be given by an infinite decimal representation.
   a. Real number23
   b. Thing
   c. Undefined
   d. Undefined

24. In mathematics, the _____ of two sets A and B is the set that contains all elements of A that also belong to B (or equivalently, all elements of B that also belong to A), but no other elements.
   a. Intersection24
   b. Thing
   c. Undefined
   d. Undefined

25. In set theory and other branches of mathematics, the _____ of a collection of sets is the set that contains everything that belongs to any of the sets, but nothing else.
   a. Thing
   b. Union25
   c. Undefined
   d. Undefined

26. In mathematics and more specifically set theory, the _____ is the unique set which contains no elements.

a. Thing
b. Empty set26
c. Undefined
d. Undefined

27. The _____, the average in everyday English, which is also called the arithmetic _____ (and is distinguished from the geometric _____ or harmonic _____). The average is also called the sample _____. The expected value of a random variable, which is also called the population _____.

a. Mean27
b. Thing
c. Undefined
d. Undefined

Chapter 3. Graphs, Relations, and Functions

1. _____ is a physical quantity expressing the size of a part of a surface. The term can also be used in a non-mathematical context to be mean "vicinity".
   a. Area1
   b. Thing
   c. Undefined
   d. Undefined

2. _____ was a highly influential French philosopher, mathematician, scientist, and writer. Dubbed the "Founder of Modern Philosophy", and the "Father of Modern Mathematics". His theories provided the basis for the calculus of Newton and Leibniz, by applying infinitesimal calculus to the tangent line problem, thus permitting the evolution of that branch of modern mathematics
   a. Descartes2
   b. Person
   c. Undefined
   d. Undefined

3. An _____ is a mathematical statement, in symbols, that two things are the same or equivalent. Equations are written with an equal sign, as in 2 + 3 = 5.
   a. Thing
   b. Equation3
   c. Undefined
   d. Undefined

4. A _____ is a symbolic representation denoting a quantity or expression. It often represents an "unknown" quantity that has the potential to change.
   a. Variable4
   b. Thing
   c. Undefined
   d. Undefined

5. In the mathematical field of graph theory, a _____ is a simple graph where an edge connects every pair of distinct vertices.
   a. Thing
   b. Complete graph5
   c. Undefined
   d. Undefined

Chapter 3. Graphs, Relations, and Functions

6. In mathematics, a _____ of a k-place relation $L \subseteq X_1 \times \ldots \times X_k$ is one of the sets X_j, $1 \leq j \leq k$. In the special case where k = 2 and $L \subseteq X_1 \times X_2$ is a function $L : X_1 \to X_2$, it is conventional to refer to X_1 as the _____ of the function and to refer to X_2 as the codomain of the function.
   a. Thing
   b. Domain6
   c. Undefined
   d. Undefined

7. In mathematics, the _____ of a function is the set of all "output" values produced by that function. Given a function $f : A \to B$, the _____ of f, is defined to be the set $\{x \in B : x = f(a)$ for some $a \in A\}$.
   a. Range7
   b. Thing
   c. Undefined
   d. Undefined

8. The mathematical concept of a _____ expresses the intuitive idea of deterministic dependence between two quantities, one of which is viewed as primary and the other as secondary. A _____ then is a way to associate a unique output for each input of a specified type, for example, a real number or an element of a given set.
   a. Function8
   b. Thing
   c. Undefined
   d. Undefined

9. In a function the _____, is the variable which is the value, i.e. the "output", of the function.
   a. Thing
   b. Dependent variable9
   c. Undefined
   d. Undefined

10. In mathematics, an _____ is any of the arguments, i.e. "inputs", to a function. Thus if we have a function f(x), then x is a _____.
    a. Independent variable10
    b. Thing
    c. Undefined
    d. Undefined

11. In plane geometry, a _____ is a polygon with four equal sides, four right angles, and parallel opposite sides. In algebra, the _____ of a number is that number multiplied by itself.
   a. Square11
   b. Thing
   c. Undefined
   d. Undefined

12. In mathematics, a _____ is a square root of a function with respect to the operation of function composition. In other words, the functional square root of a function g is a function f satisfying f(f(x)) = g(x) for all x. For example, f(x) = 2x2 is a functional square root of g(x) = 8x4.
   a. Square function12
   b. Thing
   c. Undefined
   d. Undefined

1. The word _____ comes from the Latin word linearis, which means created by lines.
    a. Thing
    b. Linear1
    c. Undefined
    d. Undefined

2. The mathematical concept of a _____ expresses the intuitive idea of deterministic dependence between two quantities, one of which is viewed as primary and the other as secondary. A _____ then is a way to associate a unique output for each input of a specified type, for example, a real number or an element of a given set.
    a. Function2
    b. Thing
    c. Undefined
    d. Undefined

3. An _____ is a mathematical statement, in symbols, that two things are the same or equivalent. Equations are written with an equal sign, as in 2 + 3 = 5.
    a. Thing
    b. Equation3
    c. Undefined
    d. Undefined

4. _____ is a notation for writing numbers that is often used by scientists and mathematicians to make it easier to write large and small numbers.
    a. Scientific notation4
    b. Thing
    c. Undefined
    d. Undefined

5. In astronomy, geography, geometry and related sciences and contexts, a plane is said to be _____ at a given point if it is locally perpendicular to the gradient of the gravity field, i.e., with the direction of the gravitational force at that point.
    a. Horizontal5
    b. Thing
    c. Undefined
    d. Undefined

Chapter 4. Linear Functions and Their Graphs

6. _____ is often used to describe the measurement of the steepness, incline, gradient, or grade of a straight line. The _____ is defined as the ratio of the "rise" divided by the "run" between two points on a line, or in other words, the ratio of the altitude change to the horizontal distance between any two points on the line.
   a. Thing
   b. Slope6
   c. Undefined
   d. Undefined

7. _____ is an Ancient Greek word meaning "power" or "force".
   a. Dunamis7
   b. Thing
   c. Undefined
   d. Undefined

8. A _____ is a special kind of ratio, indicating a relationship between two measurements with different units, such as miles to gallons or cents to pounds.
   a. Rate8
   b. Thing
   c. Undefined
   d. Undefined

9. In philosophy, mathematics, and logic, a _____ is an attribute of an object; thus a red object is said to have the _____ of redness.
   a. Property9
   b. Thing
   c. Undefined
   d. Undefined

10. The _____ expresses the fact that the difference in the y coordinate between two points on a line that is, $y - y_1$ is proportional to the difference in the x coordinate that is, $x - x_1$. The proportionality constant is m (the slope of the line.
    a. Point-slope form10
    b. Thing
    c. Undefined
    d. Undefined

11. _____ is a form where m is the slope of the line and b is the y-intercept, which is the y-coordinate of the point where the line crosses the y axis. This can be seen by letting x = 0, which immediately gives y = b.
   a. Thing
   b. Slope-intercept form11
   c. Undefined
   d. Undefined

12. The existence and properties of _____ are the basis of Euclid's parallel postulate. _____ are two lines on the same plane that do not intersect even assuming that lines extend to infinity in either direction.
   a. Parallel lines12
   b. Thing
   c. Undefined
   d. Undefined

13. _____ is either of the two parts into which a plane divides the three-dimensional space. More generally, a _____ is either of the two parts into which a hyperplane divides an affine space.
   a. Thing
   b. Half-space13
   c. Undefined
   d. Undefined

14. A _____ is a symbolic representation denoting a quantity or expression. It often represents an "unknown" quantity that has the potential to change.
   a. Thing
   b. Variable14
   c. Undefined
   d. Undefined

15. In economics, business, and accounting, a _____ is the value of money that has been used up to produce something, and hence is not available for use anymore. In business, the _____ may be one of acquisition, in which case the amount of money expended to acquire it is counted as _____.
   a. Thing
   b. Cost15
   c. Undefined
   d. Undefined

Chapter 5. Systems of Linear Equations and Inequalities

1. A _____ is a symbolic representation denoting a quantity or expression. It often represents an "unknown" quantity that has the potential to change.
   a. Variable1
   b. Thing
   c. Undefined
   d. Undefined

2. An _____ is a mathematical statement, in symbols, that two things are the same or equivalent. Equations are written with an equal sign, as in 2 + 3 = 5.
   a. Equation2
   b. Thing
   c. Undefined
   d. Undefined

3. The word _____ comes from the Latin word linearis, which means created by lines.
   a. Thing
   b. Linear3
   c. Undefined
   d. Undefined

4. The mathematical concept of a _____ expresses the intuitive idea of deterministic dependence between two quantities, one of which is viewed as primary and the other as secondary. A _____ then is a way to associate a unique output for each input of a specified type, for example, a real number or an element of a given set.
   a. Thing
   b. Function4
   c. Undefined
   d. Undefined

5. In mathematics, the _____ of two sets A and B is the set that contains all elements of A that also belong to B (or equivalently, all elements of B that also belong to A), but no other elements.
   a. Intersection5
   b. Thing
   c. Undefined
   d. Undefined

6. In mathematics, a _____ is a rectangular table of numbers or, more generally, a table consisting of abstract quantities that can be added and multiplied.

a. Matrix6
b. Thing
c. Undefined
d. Undefined

7. In plane geometry, a _____ is a polygon with four equal sides, four right angles, and parallel opposite sides. In algebra, the _____ of a number is that number multiplied by itself.
a. Thing
b. Square7
c. Undefined
d. Undefined

8. _____ is a mathematical operation, written a^n, involving two numbers, the base a and the exponent n.
a. Exponentiating8
b. Thing
c. Undefined
d. Undefined

9. The _____ governs the differentiation of products of differentiable functions.
a. Product Rule9
b. Thing
c. Undefined
d. Undefined

10. In mathematics, a _____ is the end result of a division problem. It can also be expressed as the number of times the divisor divides into the dividend.
a. Thing
b. Quotient10
c. Undefined
d. Undefined

11. Mathematical _____ is used in mathematics, and throughout the physical sciences, engineering, and economics. The complexity of such _____ ranges from relatively simple symbolic representations, such as numbers 1 and 2; function symbols sin and +, to conceptual symbols, such as lim and dy/dx; to equations and variables.

Chapter 5. Systems of Linear Equations and Inequalities

a. Notation11
b. Thing
c. Undefined
d. Undefined

Chapter 6. Polynomials and Polynomial Functions

1. In mathematics, a _____ is an expression that is constructed from one or more variables and constants, using only the operations of addition, subtraction, multiplication, and constant positive whole number exponents. is a _____. Note in particular that division by an expression containing a variable is not in general allowed in polynomials.
    a. Thing
    b. Polynomial1
    c. Undefined
    d. Undefined

2. A _____ is a symbolic representation denoting a quantity or expression. It often represents an "unknown" quantity that has the potential to change.
    a. Thing
    b. Variable2
    c. Undefined
    d. Undefined

3. An _____ is a combination of numbers, operators, grouping symbols and/or free variables and bound variables arranged in a meaningful way which can be evaluated..
    a. Thing
    b. Expression3
    c. Undefined
    d. Undefined

4. _____ is a notation for writing numbers that is often used by scientists and mathematicians to make it easier to write large and small numbers.
    a. Scientific notation4
    b. Thing
    c. Undefined
    d. Undefined

5. In astronomy, geography, geometry and related sciences and contexts, a plane is said to be _____ at a given point if it is locally perpendicular to the gradient of the gravity field, i.e., with the direction of the gravitational force at that point.
    a. Thing
    b. Horizontal5
    c. Undefined
    d. Undefined

Chapter 6. Polynomials and Polynomial Functions

6. _____ is the mathematical operation of combining or adding two numbers to obtain an equal simple amount or total.
   a. Addition6
   b. Thing
   c. Undefined
   d. Undefined

7. The word _____ comes from the Latin word linearis, which means created by lines.
   a. Linear7
   b. Thing
   c. Undefined
   d. Undefined

8. The mathematical concept of a _____ expresses the intuitive idea of deterministic dependence between two quantities, one of which is viewed as primary and the other as secondary. A _____ then is a way to associate a unique output for each input of a specified type, for example, a real number or an element of a given set.
   a. Function8
   b. Thing
   c. Undefined
   d. Undefined

9. _____ is a mathematical operation, written a^n, involving two numbers, the base a and the exponent n.
   a. Thing
   b. Exponentiating9
   c. Undefined
   d. Undefined

10. The _____ governs the differentiation of products of differentiable functions.
    a. Thing
    b. Product Rule10
    c. Undefined
    d. Undefined

11. In philosophy, mathematics, and logic, a _____ is an attribute of an object; thus a red object is said to have the _____ of redness.

a. Property11
b. Thing
c. Undefined
d. Undefined

12. The _____ is commonly taught to US high school students learning algebra as a mnemonic for remembering how to multiply two binomials.
    a. Thing
    b. FOIL rule12
    c. Undefined
    d. Undefined

13. In plane geometry, a _____ is a polygon with four equal sides, four right angles, and parallel opposite sides. In algebra, the _____ of a number is that number multiplied by itself.
    a. Thing
    b. Square13
    c. Undefined
    d. Undefined

14. In mathematics, a _____ of an integer n, also called a factor of n, is an integer which evenly divides n without leaving a remainder.
    a. Divisor14
    b. Thing
    c. Undefined
    d. Undefined

15. In mathematics, a _____ is the end result of a division problem. It can also be expressed as the number of times the divisor divides into the dividend.
    a. Thing
    b. Quotient15
    c. Undefined
    d. Undefined

16. In mathematics, _____ allows the rapid division of any polynomial by a binomial of the form x − r. It was described by Paolo Ruffini in 1809. _____ is a special case of long division when the divisor is a linear factor.

a. Thing
b. Ruffini's rule16
c. Undefined
d. Undefined

17. In mathematics, a _____ is a statement that can be proved on the basis of explicitly stated or previously agreed assumptions.
   a. Thing
   b. Theorem17
   c. Undefined
   d. Undefined

18. In mathematics the _____ refers to the identity: $a^2 - b^2 = (a+b)(a-b)$
   a. Thing
   b. Difference of two squares18
   c. Undefined
   d. Undefined

19. In the mathematical areas of algebra and analysis, the _____, is an abstract and explicit statement of the familiar property from elementary mathematics that if the product of two real numbers is zero, then at least one of the numbers in the product (factors) must be zero.
   a. Zero-Product Property19
   b. Thing
   c. Undefined
   d. Undefined

20. An _____ is a mathematical statement, in symbols, that two things are the same or equivalent. Equations are written with an equal sign, as in 2 + 3 = 5.
   a. Equation20
   b. Thing
   c. Undefined
   d. Undefined

21. In mathematics, a _____ is a polynomial equation of the second degree. The general form is $ax^2 + bx + c = 0$.

a. Quadratic equation21
b. Thing
c. Undefined
d. Undefined

22. In mathematics, the _____ is the least common multiple of the denominators of a set of vulgar fractions.
a. Thing
b. Lowest common denominator22
c. Undefined
d. Undefined

Chapter 7. Rational Expressions and Rational Functions

1. In mathematics, a _____ of a k-place relation $L \subseteq X_1 \times ... \times X_k$ is one of the sets X_j, $1 \leq j \leq k$. In the special case where k = 2 and $L \subseteq X_1 \times X_2$ is a function $L : X_1 \to X_2$, it is conventional to refer to X_1 as the _____ of the function and to refer to X_2 as the codomain of the function.
   a. Domain1
   b. Thing
   c. Undefined
   d. Undefined

2. The mathematical concept of a _____ expresses the intuitive idea of deterministic dependence between two quantities, one of which is viewed as primary and the other as secondary. A _____ then is a way to associate a unique output for each input of a specified type, for example, a real number or an element of a given set.
   a. Thing
   b. Function2
   c. Undefined
   d. Undefined

3. In mathematics, the _____ is the least common multiple of the denominators of a set of vulgar fractions.
   a. Lowest common denominator3
   b. Thing
   c. Undefined
   d. Undefined

4. The _____, the average in everyday English, which is also called the arithmetic _____ (and is distinguished from the geometric _____ or harmonic _____). The average is also called the sample _____. The expected value of a random variable, which is also called the population _____.
   a. Thing
   b. Mean4
   c. Undefined
   d. Undefined

5. An _____ is a mathematical statement, in symbols, that two things are the same or equivalent. Equations are written with an equal sign, as in 2 + 3 = 5.
   a. Thing
   b. Equation5
   c. Undefined
   d. Undefined

6. In mathematics, a _____ is a polynomial equation of the second degree. The general form is $ax^2 + bx + c = 0$.
   a. Quadratic equation6
   b. Thing
   c. Undefined
   d. Undefined

7. A _____ is a symbolic representation denoting a quantity or expression. It often represents an "unknown" quantity that has the potential to change.
   a. Thing
   b. Variable7
   c. Undefined
   d. Undefined

8. _____ is a special mathematical relationship between two quantities. Two quantities are called proportional if they vary in such a way that one of the quantities is a constant multiple of the other, or equivalently if they have a constant ratio.
   a. Thing
   b. Proportionality8
   c. Undefined
   d. Undefined

9. _____ is a function whose values do not vary and thus are constant.
   a. Constant function9
   b. Thing
   c. Undefined
   d. Undefined

10. A _____ is a special kind of ratio, indicating a relationship between two measurements with different units, such as miles to gallons or cents to pounds.
    a. Rate10
    b. Thing
    c. Undefined
    d. Undefined

11. _____ of an object is its speed in a particular direction.

Chapter 7. Rational Expressions and Rational Functions 27

a. Velocity11
b. Thing
c. Undefined
d. Undefined

12. In plane geometry, a _____ is a polygon with four equal sides, four right angles, and parallel opposite sides. In algebra, the _____ of a number is that number multiplied by itself.
  a. Thing
  b. Square12
  c. Undefined
  d. Undefined

13. In mathematics, a _____ of a number x is a number r such that r^2 = x, or in words, a number r whose square (the result of multiplying the number by itself) is x.
  a. Square root13
  b. Thing
  c. Undefined
  d. Undefined

14. In philosophy, mathematics, and logic, a _____ is an attribute of an object; thus a red object is said to have the _____ of redness.
  a. Property14
  b. Thing
  c. Undefined
  d. Undefined

15. In mathematics, a _____ of a complex-valued function f is a member x of the domain of f such that f(x) vanishes at x, that is, x : f (x) = 0.
  a. Root15
  b. Thing
  c. Undefined
  d. Undefined

16. In mathematics, a _____ may be described informally as a number that can be given by an infinite decimal representation.

a. Real number16
b. Thing
c. Undefined
d. Undefined

Chapter 8. Radicals and Rational Exponents

1. A _____ of a number is a number a such that $a^3 = x$.
   a. Cube root1
   b. Thing
   c. Undefined
   d. Undefined

2. In mathematics, a _____ of a complex-valued function f is a member x of the domain of f such that f(x) vanishes at x, that is, x : f (x) = 0.
   a. Root2
   b. Thing
   c. Undefined
   d. Undefined

3. In plane geometry, a _____ is a polygon with four equal sides, four right angles, and parallel opposite sides. In algebra, the _____ of a number is that number multiplied by itself.
   a. Thing
   b. Square3
   c. Undefined
   d. Undefined

4. _____ is a mathematical operation, written a^n, involving two numbers, the base a and the exponent n.
   a. Exponentiating4
   b. Thing
   c. Undefined
   d. Undefined

5. _____ is an inexact representation of something that is still close enough to be useful. Although approximation is most often applied to numbers, it is also frequently applied to such things as mathematical functions, shapes, and physical laws.
   a. Thing
   b. Approximating5
   c. Undefined
   d. Undefined

6. The _____ governs the differentiation of products of differentiable functions.

a. Thing
b. Product Rule6
c. Undefined
d. Undefined

7. In mathematics, a _____ is the end result of a division problem. It can also be expressed as the number of times the divisor divides into the dividend.
   a. Thing
   b. Quotient7
   c. Undefined
   d. Undefined

8. A _____ is an expression containing a square root.
   a. Thing
   b. Radical expression8
   c. Undefined
   d. Undefined

9. In philosophy, mathematics, and logic, a _____ is an attribute of an object; thus a red object is said to have the _____ of redness.
   a. Property9
   b. Thing
   c. Undefined
   d. Undefined

10. A _____ is a symbolic representation denoting a quantity or expression. It often represents an "unknown" quantity that has the potential to change.
    a. Thing
    b. Variable10
    c. Undefined
    d. Undefined

11. In mathematics, a _____ of a number x is a number r such that $r^2 = x$, or in words, a number r whose square (the result of multiplying the number by itself) is x.

a. Thing
b. Square root11
c. Undefined
d. Undefined

12. The mathematical concept of a _____ expresses the intuitive idea of deterministic dependence between two quantities, one of which is viewed as primary and the other as secondary. A _____ then is a way to associate a unique output for each input of a specified type, for example, a real number or an element of a given set.
   a. Function12
   b. Thing
   c. Undefined
   d. Undefined

13. In mathematics, a _____ of a k-place relation $L \subseteq X_1 \times ... \times X_k$ is one of the sets X_j, $1 \leq j \leq k$. In the special case where k = 2 and $L \subseteq X_1 \times X_2$ is a function $L : X_1 \to X_2$, it is conventional to refer to X_1 as the _____ of the function and to refer to X_2 as the codomain of the function.
   a. Thing
   b. Domain13
   c. Undefined
   d. Undefined

14. An _____ is a mathematical statement, in symbols, that two things are the same or equivalent. Equations are written with an equal sign, as in 2 + 3 = 5.
   a. Equation14
   b. Thing
   c. Undefined
   d. Undefined

15. In mathematics, a _____ is a number in the form of a + bi where a and b are real numbers, and i is the imaginary unit, with the property i 2 = −1. The real number a is called the real part of the _____, and the real number b is the imaginary part.
   a. Complex number15
   b. Thing
   c. Undefined
   d. Undefined

16. _____ is a notation for writing numbers that is often used by scientists and mathematicians to make it easier to write large and small numbers.
   a. Thing
   b. Scientific notation16
   c. Undefined
   d. Undefined

17. In mathematics, a _____ may be described informally as a number that can be given by an infinite decimal representation.
   a. Real number17
   b. Thing
   c. Undefined
   d. Undefined

Chapter 9. Quadratic Equations and Functions

1. In philosophy, mathematics, and logic, a _____ is an attribute of an object; thus a red object is said to have the _____ of redness.
   a. Property1
   b. Thing
   c. Undefined
   d. Undefined

2. In mathematics, a _____ is a polynomial equation of the second degree. The general form is $ax^2 + bx + c = 0$.
   a. Thing
   b. Quadratic equation2
   c. Undefined
   d. Undefined

3. In mathematics, a _____ of a complex-valued function f is a member x of the domain of f such that f(x) vanishes at x, that is, $x : f(x) = 0$.
   a. Root3
   b. Thing
   c. Undefined
   d. Undefined

4. In plane geometry, a _____ is a polygon with four equal sides, four right angles, and parallel opposite sides. In algebra, the _____ of a number is that number multiplied by itself.
   a. Square4
   b. Thing
   c. Undefined
   d. Undefined

5. In mathematics, a _____ of a number x is a number r such that $r^2 = x$, or in words, a number r whose square (the result of multiplying the number by itself) is x.
   a. Square Root5
   b. Thing
   c. Undefined
   d. Undefined

6. An _____ is a mathematical statement, in symbols, that two things are the same or equivalent. Equations are written with an equal sign, as in $2 + 3 = 5$.

Chapter 9. Quadratic Equations and Functions

    a. Thing
    b. Equation6
    c. Undefined
    d. Undefined

7. A _____ is a symbolic representation denoting a quantity or expression. It often represents an "unknown" quantity that has the potential to change.
    a. Variable7
    b. Thing
    c. Undefined
    d. Undefined

8. In geometry and trigonometry, a _____ is defined as an angle between two straight intersecting lines of ninety degrees, or one-quarter of a circle.
    a. Thing
    b. Right angle8
    c. Undefined
    d. Undefined

9. In mathematics, a _____ is a statement that can be proved on the basis of explicitly stated or previously agreed assumptions.
    a. Theorem9
    b. Thing
    c. Undefined
    d. Undefined

10. A quadratic equation with real solutions, called roots, which may be real or complex, is given by the _____: $x = {-b \pm \sqrt{b^2 - 4ac} \over 2a}$.
    a. Thing
    b. Quadratic formula10
    c. Undefined
    d. Undefined

11. The mathematical concept of a _____ expresses the intuitive idea of deterministic dependence between two quantities, one of which is viewed as primary and the other as secondary. A _____ then is a way to associate a unique output for each input of a specified type, for example, a real number or an element of a given set.

a. Function11
b. Thing
c. Undefined
d. Undefined

12. In mathematics, the _____ is a conic section generated by the intersection of a right circular conical surface and a plane parallel to a generating straight line of that surface. It can also be defined as locus of points in a plane which are equidistant from a given point.
   a. Thing
   b. Parabola12
   c. Undefined
   d. Undefined

13. In geometry, a _____ is a special kind of point, usually a corner of a polygon, polyhedron, or higher dimensional polytope. In the geometry of curves a _____ is a point of where the first derivative of curvature is zero. In graph theory, a _____ is the fundamental unit out of which graphs are formed
   a. Vertex13
   b. Thing
   c. Undefined
   d. Undefined

Chapter 10, Exponential and Logarithmic Functions

1. The mathematical concept of a _____ expresses the intuitive idea of deterministic dependence between two quantities, one of which is viewed as primary and the other as secondary. A _____ then is a way to associate a unique output for each input of a specified type, for example, a real number or an element of a given set.
   a. Thing
   b. Function1
   c. Undefined
   d. Undefined

2. In astronomy, geography, geometry and related sciences and contexts, a plane is said to be _____ at a given point if it is locally perpendicular to the gradient of the gravity field, i.e., with the direction of the gravitational force at that point.
   a. Horizontal2
   b. Thing
   c. Undefined
   d. Undefined

3. An _____ is a function which does the reverse of a given function.
   a. Inverse function3
   b. Thing
   c. Undefined
   d. Undefined

4. In mathematics, the _____ of a function is the set of all "output" values produced by that function. Given a function $f : A \to B$, the _____ of f, is defined to be the set $\{x \in B : x = f(a) \text{ for some } a \in A\}$.
   a. Thing
   b. Range4
   c. Undefined
   d. Undefined

5. In mathematics, a _____ of a k-place relation $L \subseteq X_1 \times \ldots \times X_k$ is one of the sets X_j, $1 \leq j \leq k$. In the special case where k = 2 and $L \subseteq X_1 \times X_2$ is a function $L : X_1 \to X_2$, it is conventional to refer to X_1 as the _____ of the function and to refer to X_2 as the codomain of the function.
   a. Thing
   b. Domain5
   c. Undefined
   d. Undefined

Chapter 10. Exponential and Logarithmic Functions

6. An _____ is a mathematical statement, in symbols, that two things are the same or equivalent. Equations are written with an equal sign, as in 2 + 3 = 5.
   a. Thing
   b. Equation6
   c. Undefined
   d. Undefined

7. _____ is one of the most important functions in mathematics. A function commonly used to study growth and decay
   a. Thing
   b. Exponential function7
   c. Undefined
   d. Undefined

8. In philosophy, mathematics, and logic, a _____ is an attribute of an object; thus a red object is said to have the _____ of redness.
   a. Thing
   b. Property8
   c. Undefined
   d. Undefined

9. _____ is the chance that something is likely to happen or be the case.
   a. Probability9
   b. Thing
   c. Undefined
   d. Undefined

10. In mathematics, a _____ of a number x is the exponent y of the power by such that $x = b^y$. The value used for the base b must be neither 0 nor 1, nor a root of 1 in the case of the extension to complex numbers, and is typically 10, e, or 2.
    a. Thing
    b. Logarithm10
    c. Undefined
    d. Undefined

11. _____ is the quality of a sound that is the primary psychological correlate of physical strength.

Chapter 10. Exponential and Logarithmic Functions

    a. Thing
    b. Loudness11
    c. Undefined
    d. Undefined

12. The _____ governs the differentiation of products of differentiable functions.
    a. Product Rule12
    b. Thing
    c. Undefined
    d. Undefined

13. In mathematics, a _____ is the end result of a division problem. It can also be expressed as the number of times the divisor divides into the dividend.
    a. Thing
    b. Quotient13
    c. Undefined
    d. Undefined

14. _____ is an inexact representation of something that is still close enough to be useful. Although approximation is most often applied to numbers, it is also frequently applied to such things as mathematical functions, shapes, and physical laws.
    a. Approximating14
    b. Thing
    c. Undefined
    d. Undefined

Chapter 11. Conics

1. Johannes Kepler's _____ contains the results of the astronomer's ten-year long investigation of the motion of Mars.
   a. Thing
   b. Astronomia nova1
   c. Undefined
   d. Undefined

2. In mathematics, a _____ is a statement that can be proved on the basis of explicitly stated or previously agreed assumptions.
   a. Thing
   b. Theorem2
   c. Undefined
   d. Undefined

3. In Euclidean geometry, a _____ is the set of all points in a plane at a fixed distance, called the radius, from a given point, the center.
   a. Thing
   b. Circle3
   c. Undefined
   d. Undefined

4. In mathematics, the _____ is a conic section generated by the intersection of a right circular conical surface and a plane parallel to a generating straight line of that surface. It can also be defined as locus of points in a plane which are equidistant from a given point.
   a. Parabola4
   b. Thing
   c. Undefined
   d. Undefined

5. In classical geometry, a _____ of a circle or sphere is any line segment from its center to its boundary. By extension, the _____ of a circle or sphere is the length of any such segment. The _____ is half the diameter. In science and engineering the term _____ of curvature is commonly used as a synonym for _____.
   a. Thing
   b. Radius5
   c. Undefined
   d. Undefined

6. An _____ is a mathematical statement, in symbols, that two things are the same or equivalent. Equations are written with an equal sign, as in 2 + 3 = 5.
   a. Thing
   b. Equation6
   c. Undefined
   d. Undefined

7. _____ is a notation for writing numbers that is often used by scientists and mathematicians to make it easier to write large and small numbers.
   a. Thing
   b. Scientific notation7
   c. Undefined
   d. Undefined

8. In geometry, a _____ is a special kind of point, usually a corner of a polygon, polyhedron, or higher dimensional polytope. In the geometry of curves a _____ is a point of where the first derivative of curvature is zero. In graph theory, a _____ is the fundamental unit out of which graphs are formed
   a. Vertex8
   b. Thing
   c. Undefined
   d. Undefined

9. In geometry, the _____ are a pair of special points used in describing conic sections. The four types of conic sections are the circle, parabola, ellipse, and hyperbola.
   a. Foci9
   b. Thing
   c. Undefined
   d. Undefined

10. The _____, the average in everyday English, which is also called the arithmetic _____ (and is distinguished from the geometric _____ or harmonic _____). The average is also called the sample _____. The expected value of a random variable, which is also called the population _____.
    a. Thing
    b. Mean10
    c. Undefined
    d. Undefined

11. An _____ is a straight line or curve A to which another curve B approaches closer and closer as one moves along it. As one moves along B, the space between it and the _____ A becomes smaller and smaller, and can in fact be made as small as one could wish by going far enough along. A curve may or may not touch or cross its _____. In fact, the curve may intersect the _____ an infinite number of times.
   a. Thing
   b. Asymptote11
   c. Undefined
   d. Undefined

Chapter 12. Sequences, Series, and the Binomial Theorem

1. Mathematical _____ is used in mathematics, and throughout the physical sciences, engineering, and economics. The complexity of such _____ ranges from relatively simple symbolic representations, such as numbers 1 and 2; function symbols sin and +, to conceptual symbols, such as lim and dy/dx; to equations and variables.
    a. Thing
    b. Notation1
    c. Undefined
    d. Undefined

2. _____ is the mathematical operation of combining or adding two numbers to obtain an equal simple amount or total.
    a. Thing
    b. Addition2
    c. Undefined
    d. Undefined

3. _____ is a kind of property which exists as magnitude or multitude. It is among the basic classes of things along with quality, substance, change, and relation.
    a. Thing
    b. Amount3
    c. Undefined
    d. Undefined

4. In mathematics, a _____ is a statement that can be proved on the basis of explicitly stated or previously agreed assumptions.
    a. Theorem4
    b. Thing
    c. Undefined
    d. Undefined

5. In mathematics, a _____ is an expression that is constructed from one or more variables and constants, using only the operations of addition, subtraction, multiplication, and constant positive whole number exponents. is a _____. Note in particular that division by an expression containing a variable is not in general allowed in polynomials.
    a. Polynomial5
    b. Thing
    c. Undefined
    d. Undefined

Chapter 12. Sequences, Series, and the Binomial Theorem

6. The _____ governs the differentiation of products of differentiable functions.
   a. Product Rule6
   b. Thing
   c. Undefined
   d. Undefined

7. In mathematics, a _____ is the end result of a division problem. It can also be expressed as the number of times the divisor divides into the dividend.
   a. Thing
   b. Quotient7
   c. Undefined
   d. Undefined

8. In mathematics, the _____ is a conic section generated by the intersection of a right circular conical surface and a plane parallel to a generating straight line of that surface. It can also be defined as locus of points in a plane which are equidistant from a given point.
   a. Thing
   b. Parabola8
   c. Undefined
   d. Undefined

Chapter 1
1. b 2. a 3. b 4. a 5. a 6. a 7. a 8. a 9. b 10. a
11. a 12. b 13. b 14. a 15. b 16. b 17. b 18. a 19. a

Chapter 2
1. a 2. b 3. a 4. b 5. a 6. b 7. b 8. a 9. a 10. b
11. b 12. a 13. a 14. b 15. b 16. b 17. b 18. b 19. b 20. a
21. a 22. b 23. a 24. a 25. b 26. b 27. a

Chapter 3
1. a 2. a 3. b 4. a 5. b 6. b 7. a 8. a 9. b 10. a
11. a 12. a

Chapter 4
1. b 2. a 3. b 4. a 5. a 6. b 7. a 8. a 9. a 10. a
11. b 12. a 13. b 14. b 15. b

Chapter 5
1. a 2. a 3. b 4. b 5. a 6. a 7. b 8. a 9. a 10. b
11. a

Chapter 6
1. b 2. b 3. b 4. a 5. b 6. a 7. a 8. a 9. b 10. b
11. a 12. b 13. b 14. a 15. b 16. b 17. b 18. b 19. a 20. a
21. a 22. b

Chapter 7
1. a 2. b 3. a 4. b 5. b 6. a 7. b 8. b 9. a 10. a
11. a 12. b 13. a 14. a 15. a 16. a

Chapter 8
1. a 2. a 3. b 4. a 5. b 6. b 7. b 8. b 9. a 10. b
11. b 12. a 13. b 14. a 15. a 16. b 17. a

Chapter 9
1. a 2. b 3. a 4. a 5. a 6. b 7. a 8. b 9. a 10. b
11. a 12. b 13. a

Chapter 10
1. b 2. a 3. a 4. b 5. b 6. b 7. b 8. b 9. a 10. b
11. b 12. a 13. b 14. a

Chapter 11
1. b 2. b 3. b 4. a 5. b 6. b 7. b 8. a 9. a 10. b
11. b

ANSWER KEY

Chapter 12
1. b   2. b   3. b   4. a   5. a   6. a   7. b   8. b

www.ingramcontent.com/pod-product-compliance
Lightning Source LLC
Chambersburg PA
CBHW081220230426
43666CB00015B/2818